SILVER AND
INFORMATION

Books by Bruce Smith

The Common Wages
Silver and Information
Mercy Seat
The Other Lover
Songs for Two Voices
Devotions
Spill

Silver and Information

poems by
Bruce Smith

Carnegie Mellon University Press
Pittsburgh 2020

Cover design: Faith Kim

Library of Congress Control Number: 2018940314
ISBN: 978-0-88748-645-6
Copyright © 1985 by Bruce Smith
All rights reserved
Printed and bound in the United States of America

10 9 8 7 6 5 4 3 2 1

Silver and Information was first published by the University of
Georgia Press, Athens, Georgia, in 1985.

First Carnegie Mellon University Press Classic Contemporaries
Edition, February 2020

FOR PETER BALAKIAN

Acknowledgments

Grateful acknowledgment is made to the following publications in which these poems have appeared:

New England Review / Bread Loaf Quarterly: "Address," "Diabetes," "In My Father's House," "Testimony," "O My Invisible Estate," "Visitation," "Faulty Story," "Laundry," "My Father Moves," "Misdemeanor," "The Failure of His Economy," "Window"

The Nation: "Silver and Information," "Black Ducks," "Calm"

American Poetry Review: "The Woman in Me," "One Note Rage Can Understand"

Shenandoah: "The Higher Beauties"

Yarrow: "A Small Sing of My Cupidity"

Crazy Horse: "It Was Foul and I Loved It," "The Ocean"

Poetry: "Snow on the Ocean"

Times Literary Supplement: "This Can't Be," "Salary"

New Republic: "Geometry and Sea Air"

The poems in Part One appeared in *Invisible Estate* (Appletree Alley Press, 1984). "Window" appeared in *Divided Light: Father and Son Poems,* edited by Jason Shinder (Sheep Meadow Press, 1983). *The debt immense of endless gratitude* to the Fine Arts Work Center in Provincetown and, once again, to Jack Wheatcroft.

Contents

I

Address 3
This Can't Be 4
You Cannot Solder an Abyss with Air 5
Basement 6
Nail 7
Salary 8
Diabetes 9
In My Father's House 10
Testimony 11
St. Elmo 12
O My Invisible Estate 13
Visitation 14
Faulty Story 15
Laundry 16
My Father Moves 17
Misdemeanor 18
The Failure of His Economy 19
Window 20

II

Silver and Information 23
It Was Foul and I Loved It 25
One Note Rage Can Understand 26
The Ocean 27
Calm 29
Half Wish 30
Snow on the Ocean 31

Black Ducks   32
The Woman in Me   34
What the Sea Feeds Us   36
After the Storm   38
Swan's Riding   39

III

Geometry and Sea Air   45
The Higher Beauties   47
Signorelli's *Last Judgment*, the Blessed   48
Rooms of Ingres   49
Eyes   50
A Small Sing of My Cupidity   53
Meridian Street   54
When the Rapture Comes   56
Ode   58

I

Address

Street of Nectar, Street of Contingency,
Street of Fecundity like the moon's sea.
Street of First Kissing, Street of the Franchise,
Street of Some Money where his house is.
Boulevard of the Boy-in-Summer Rising
into the Sun. Street of Small Gashes
where his house is. Street of the Plangent,
Street of the Whips of Plantain, Place
of Illuminated Mother, Street of the Fallen
Motorcycle Cop, The Lane of One-Accounted-For,
Road of Want-More. Street of Rose Agony
where his house is. Concourse of the Party,
Street Impolitic, Street of Circumference, Wheel, Disc, Arc.
Street of Moonlighting, Street of His Tendons, Street of Duress,
Street of His Mansions, Street of His Sweetness, numberless.

This Can't Be

the place of consequence, the station of his embrace.
Or else I'm not son enough to see
the innocence and the spiritual fiddlings
in the uneven floorboards and joists,
in the guttural speech of the pipes,
in the limp and the lack of heat.
All we need, all we really need is light!
And let there be a roof with no leaks.
Oh father landlord, fill up all our breaches.

He gives himself to the cracks; into the chinks
my father lowers his bone,
the do-it-yourself funeral. He holds the wires
in his teeth. He strips the insulation back.
If it's black, it's juiceless; if it's red, elegiac.

You Cannot Solder an Abyss with Air

—DICKINSON

He fixes it. He walks the spinal stair
that snaps his back, the lath and plaster seal
him as he lies in it. He beats one in.
What he hears is the skin's thinness.
He hears the echo of his whereabouts, his end.
Tin flashing over things conspiring to ignore him
for sucking all our jesus in.
This white engine of our fullness
sputters in the sweetness
of his meat. He hears . . . he hears what's near
and useful, a cold chisel, claw hammer, wrench.

Sure, I'll make the floor bare for him.
I'll make the rat-black shingles burst
the supplies of his desire; I'll provide.

Basement

Somewhere between the source of lightning
and the dust, beneath the staircase where
our likenesses are hung, there
my father works at the afflicted basis of our building.

No clock, no calendar
with poses of the rainbow trout against the aquamarine
backdrop. No cheesecake glossies, gaps between
tits and ass, although his vessels are hard
with the force of his blood. The mean,
dark places where you learned the strange things
that a man might do among those cloudy fluorescent
tubes that lit splinters and the silver shards and sent
light through us, filled us, fixed us, bent, magnificent.

Nail

What makes the nails come loose?
he asks me, deep in his basement.
With the first jerk—a groan from the hammer's noose,
the body releases its hold. Cool, spent,
will-less to the second pull into air
where it sighs and rises, he says,
mystic at sixty. There are
the ways of nail and there are the ways
of worm that come closer to him—
the white, blank target in the mud.
His way is to settle with the day as things leave him
with his sight as the blood
pulls him downward in the darkness of the self
where no rat bites, no worm affirms the pulse.

Salary

The working class and the employing class have nothing
in common—my father's wobbly preamble,
his variance with the world, a little union man, a little
Joe Hill who lived, which means losing less than all,
which means gambling and losing the luxury of gambling,
which means a salary of white bread and butter, ampules
of insulin, just covering his ass by that industry
of debit and credit at the blood school.

I figured his expenditure in song:
the cherry his love gave him without a stone,
the chicken his love gave him that had no bone.
Sums of nothing, balance of nothing. To belong
to this man, two Christs old, is to sing for him
the staggering bill, a son, *a baby with no cryin'.*

Diabetes

In Philadelphia, a Sunday, my father lying
on the davenport, his head cocked
to look above the painting of a woman playing
the baroque organ. In the silent Bach,
in the voluptuous folds of her maroon
gown, I found out about my father's sweetness.

The same sugar I'm immune to,
except for the holes it makes in my teeth,
can make a hole of my father
by carrying him off in his water
so he becomes the creases in her rich fabric,
the air in the long barrels of the organ. Hollow,
but no one knows . . . I know, I know: a sweetness
that empties, an emptiness that overflows.

In My Father's House

In my father's house are the rooms of his undoing.
If it were not so I would have told you.
The blue-black nail and the knots of his unnaming
and the blackness under his nail and the blue
thumb from the hammer's arc and the sparks
that bite blue moons in the ends of all his tools.
And the dangerous stars he sees there in the dark.
And the belly he's worked hard at and the foolish
place he lies down in with such sweetness that he must
be made from other stuff than this.
The floor he walks on holds him
and the ceiling has no hooks
when he passes through his sweet unrest
and our hundred natural shocks.

Testimony

Now he's reading Raymond Chandler in the dark house.
. . . with the sound a bill makes in a wallet
she uncrosses her legs . . . he awakes south
of Newark, his gun gone with his cigarettes,
his left elbow's in front of his face for a lifetime,
he's crapped out on all his bets. And the thigh
that he strokes is his own. To this crime,
and to his silent rioting, I testify.
And the shudders I am heir to
and the fists within my chest
and the Quaker quietism
and the bloody tenderness
and the plots of our misgiving
and our same names, anonymous.

St. Elmo

And his name, anonymous, around his wrist
in the hospital gown that makes him
a thin medieval saint or a beat novelist—
the words burnt into him.
His demons have their sleep
under his sheets, in his creases, so his familiar
speaks for him from deep
within the cool drink of sugar
his arm takes: *I give up my influence*
it says to me in drips from the IV.

They want to make his insides shine, hence
barium, like a clockface so we can see
the aura of his coils, the astral fire
in the works that won't expire.

O My Invisible Estate

—VAUGHAN

Where the afternoon sun blears the city.
Where the high-numbered streets zero
their dignity, we live without irony.
No house but a shadow
of a house, but when we need a shadow
this shadow is ours. The shadow
of a man and his two arms, tenderness
and some hunger that I was rocked in.
And whatever house has been in me since then,
a flesh made and unmade since then,
I find that every churchyard has a stone
that bears our name, Father. Imagine
the monuments to a name so common,
imagine that dark land is what we own.

Visitation

Just as I sit down with my father,
just as I raise one of his swollen arms
and he curls against me, stubbly, from behind
and guides my thick pencil in rows
of cursive ooooooo's
he learned to make perfect
from years of steering the wrists
of the interloper third graders.
When we move on to p's and q's
the room still hums with his n's and o's.
Son and father, father and son
     and a bat flashes before me
     in a course like a cardiac chart.
     The father darkens, a scribbled eclipse of the heart.

Faulty Story

Our summer, dusk, heat. A bite into the bruise
of the peach, our obligation. Our green leans
into the night-reaches, what we lose
our eyes to. The rhythm and blues conceits of our teens
cruise by, we can take their pulse from here.

I know how I'm injured by this history,
this insult to the body in the form of a stroke where
the cup of the skull fills with blood and we
are mute as the dark water rises in the room.
I know these war-baby legs prop a murmuring heart

and in my night sweat is that fluent man who
maims and lullabies me. The summer dark
receives these songs and grievances as our noblest organ
pumps the faulty story of my generation.

Laundry

Not even the cops who can do anything could do this—
work on Sunday picking up dirty and delivering clean
laundry in Philadelphia. Rambling with my father, get this,
in a truck that wasn't even our own,
part ambulance, part bullet, there wasn't anything
we couldn't do. Sheets of stigmata, macula of love,
vomit and shit and the stains of pissing
another week's salary away, we picked up and drove
to the stick men in shirt sleeves, the thin
Bolshevik Jews who laughed out the sheets like the empty
speech in cartoons. They smelled better than sin,
better than decadent capitalism. And oh, we
could deliver, couldn't we, the lawless bags through the city
that said in his yawn, get money, get money, get money.

My Father Moves

in the gold circle of the sealed beam
along a road lined with dream elms and maples,
a willow. The tips that he made waiting tables
ring in the shoe box—his estate—with the limes
and the galvanic lemons. The sugar
on the swizzle sticks shines for me,
emblems of his moonlighting. He's singing
"The Big Rock Candy Mountain." He nods
into the sweetness of tomorrow
where there's rubber-toothed dogs, cops
with wooden legs, where his sweet blood won't follow
the water from his body. . . . There can be no song
as shiftless as a man's song the moment before
the night stops him and the wind dents
his sleep. There can be no song that poor.

Misdemeanor

In the brand new Ford driving, his piece of faulty earth,
the Great Experiment, America. I sat on his right
wiling the engine, inventing the nervous birth
of something under the midnight
blue of the hood. I saw a house of red coals
where men burned and made their perfume,
their figures of speech. I cut down the phone poles
with an eye, I fused the city with its doom.

Inside, all I saw was his jaw, taut, his elbow,
skeletal. We ran a light in front of Blood of Our Lord
Elementary School, and the cop bellowed
us over. You squirmed and whined. I swore
I'd turn my eye on you. I burned. Driving
away, driving on. Now I forgive you everything.

The Failure of His Economy

Presently I gave up the notion of becoming President.
If anyone would ask, I would become my father.
I would be the poor be-boppist, eloquent
saxophone player in the dance band, moonlighter
that he was, if that meant being struck by moonlight,
if that meant my lips on the wheezy reed
and singing nights in smoky places flights
of scat calculated in fahrenheit and beads
of sweat, not in the currency of daylight,
the not-gold, not-hot, creased grey and green
where they printed the faces of men like Washington.

One day he threw a fistful of bills to the ceiling
and they came down on us with their inadequate wings
beating to keep those notes from falling, to keep imagining.

Window

There is a story so true, so becoming, so full of duty
and engraved love that it's glass—
a brittle crazy thing to see a father through.
It's like this: my father made a hole in the second story,
chipping the brick the way a wasp hits the glass.
He had an idea. He had a vision of a view
of Philadelphia that I couldn't see through.
I can see him tapping with a hammer
at the house, making a space for the wind,
then his hand, then enough to perch his thin body
on, working and fuming in the red brick dust, enamored
of his husbandry, when he fell headfirst into the line
my mother strung for clothes, righted himself before his destiny,
brushed himself off, became the window, the stain in the glass,
   the irony.

II

Silver and Information

An obituary has more news than this day,
brilliant, acid yellow and silver
off the water at land's end. The disparate
prismatic things blind you as they fin
their way across the surface of the water.
This light cannot inform you of your dying.

Fish of lustrous nothing, fish of desire,
fish whose push and syllable
can make things happen,
fish whose ecstatic hunger
is no longer news, and fish whose mouth
zeroes the multitudes, the hosts
who wait for their analogies
and something nice to eat, the billions
the waves commemorate in their breaking
down to their knees on the shore,
their cloacal sound. Now
how can I stay singular?
How can even one part die
when I split and split
like the smallest animal
in the ocean until I'm famous
in my dismemberment, splendid
in my hunger, and anonymous—
so that naming one
is like naming one runnel
the sea, or one drop of blood
the intoxicating passion?

I keep the multitudes in mind
when I hear daily that one

has murdered another. A news
more silver than given,
more light than anything
captured. And I hold them all
in mind—the fulgence, the data,
and the death, or else I lose it,
that package of slippery fish,
that don't die exactly but smell
in a heaven so low we can hear
the moans and feel the circles
and bite in each cell.

It Was Foul and I Loved It

—AUGUSTINE

The sea is absolute in this:
no high society, no hymen, no new rich.
Each beautiful face it wools and etches
in its double time—and what's worse,
we carry this oblivion
within us, sappy and precious
as the tattooed heart of Mother.
You'd think we could be less ruthless
in this condition—salined
and sucked out—an urge
aborted, desire's half-eaten
sweet-cake. You'd imagine
there would be less swagger,
fewer airs. But we're pulled
from our best intentions by the sea
with its terrible averages,
its long division carried out
to the numberless place.
We can't remember: are we the sea,
the fiercest self-gratifier,
or are we what's tossed and spilled,
fragrant and inflamed, the shameless
thing that's always in a lather?
It kisses everybody's ass.
It loves what stinks. Fish
shit in it. We eat the fish.

One Note Rage Can Understand

—LOUISE BOGAN

To reduce the monster to myself,
in order to scratch where it itches,
I go down to the water and listen
for my name in the waves of the bay.
I go down with the commonest surname
and half my allotted threescore years
and ten to hear what I can
in the concussive thuds off Race Point
at the cusp of America. In the agitation,
in the perjuries, in the gnats and flies,
in the middle of my life
at land's end, I hear
the churned other word.
Whose, it sounds like,
or *bruise*—a question in the descent,
an erasing statement in the sweep
back to sea that is nothing
but the breath tuned to groans
then cushioned in the utterance
by all we stand on, an anxious
susurrus of history and crushing
rhapsody that is not my name or yours.

The Ocean

hurrahing for no good reason.
The tools to know it
blown apart by its murderous frisson.
The tools to talk about it
caught in the tide
that is foaming and sighing
in sounds so absolute
that it must be homicide
or a great creamy remaking.

The shore is the story
of our disposition—how we give up
our sordid excellence. I can see
our bias in the broken ribs
of scallop and the carcasses of skate—
vertebrae and slick cartilage,
those satanic cases for its black
egg. There's a certain tendency
in the jellyfish fetus, the invisible
flagellants, the shards of whelk, tulip, moon.
Can you tell if this is the wake
and burial or a wedding
of something and all the dirtless
earth? Who knows
what to make of the cords
of tangled kelp, those blue-green
tresses? And just how political
are the shattered mirrors
and the unbound treaties
of wampum in the quahog shell?

Among the carnage and the lime,
among the human welter and harry,
junk of the prodigal,
rummage of our cups,
there are lobes of milky quartz
so beautiful you must
put them in your mouth
until your speech will be stentorian
as the sea's or tender enough
to call the lugworm from the mud.
And there are those dark stones
you take for your sensual spouse.

Calm

A moment without generation.
Silver and Elysium
when the microscopic pause
before their barely visible kill
and the smelt nuzzle their bubbles.
The mackerel relax their suicidal course
to the gullet of tuna
and tuna swim in the sea
ignorant of the open mouth of man.

In this moment of opulence
and hunger, a moment more lyrical
than miserable, your senses leap
from five to seven to ten.
Good riddance to thought, goodbye
salt and skeleton, you feel the rational
mud and rapture, the spawning
from the spaces between two breaths.

Half Wish

Fog. Headlong in the wet
direction, the wrong one

you've fallen in. Just how myopic are you?
Eyes like a child's, blind

to anything but milk,
milk that spills the sunlight

like your black mud wipes away the moon.
On either hand only the imagined

land, inelegant, cold. You can't see
your hands, the smell is vaginal,

the world's no breast, even with this near-
sightedness; you can't remember being

kissed like this. Usually you're cold,
ridiculous like the rest, defenseless

starfish of a man, a sponge, a forked
shortsighted thing with a head, half water

half wish to fall softly,
to be squeezed in the passages again.

Snow on the Ocean

You can prepare for the fall,
its lack of innocence, its bright load,
as if in the scheme of things
you've been given something—
these accomplishments
of air before the cold
paradise of winter
where no fruit falls.
You can prepare all summer for this
and the extravagant chemical changes—
the maple flaming scarlet to rust
to what? It's beneath you
to see its apostasy, its folding.
You can prepare for this
hanging and appleing

but not for this: snow
on the ocean, water in all three forms—
ghost, glass, and what slips
between our fingers, what dissolves
and hugs our forms. Just this much—
a splash in a shot glass,
an inch in a bath, the human
lull and relish of it—
can leave us beautifully used,
almost shoreless, as we pass through
the gills of this planet
with the wrong name,
this earth, whose one season
is the improvident presence of water.

Black Ducks

When the sea is this
grey, motionless, cold, eloquent
as a cough with just a bight
of ice at this edge, I think
this is just the whole skeptical works
lapsed from heaven to a labor
in sleep. The drop into the sea
of the gull is certainly not
the glide of angels. I think
there are no angels, although
they fill our letters
with their flutters and sighs, although
their furious alphabet has been described
in our bones. Consider the hands—
their tenuousness, their aptitude
for making a word rise
in the mouth of another,
ah, or the twin wings of the hips
and the incalculable bones
in the ear whose reckoning
makes this rending of air
again possible.

I think I can almost
listen to myself listen
with the minor authority
of one who has no flying
thing inside him. I grow cold,
my hands mottled—veinous blue
and white—as manifest as the wintering
ducks in the bay, as clear as the sea

is boneless and its good dullness
is a paraphrase for sleep—
look, how it rouses now,
tosses and mutters and look,
the chaotic treading
of something, something I can almost
hear beneath the surface.

for Claudia Thomas

The Woman in Me

All I have in me is the ten or twelve
characters that make up a man. The letters of my name,
a jury of my peers. And I swear
it's not the Murderer and it's not the vocal Mud
that rises up in me in the lash of winter,
it's the sad womanly one
that the Angel and the Authority
incessantly shout down. The one that sees
ice floes on the chest of the ocean,
the great non-heart beating.
The world is fluent grief, the woman in me
thinks for all of us, for the mob in the heart:
Orpheus, Absolute Dog, the Woolgatherer,
the Sheep, Virgin Father, Son.

And when we sit down together,
it's with her in my throat that I speak:
the sea scars the beaches,
the day lunges against me.
The drink that the fisherman and I take
is not the adequate figure of water's work
on us. I'd give almost anything
to have one drink be the storm, the boredom,
the shimmering profusion and the dream.
The light through these green bottles
even she would think is beautiful
but a drink and a half away
from the thrash and swell of the sea.

It's a brief Antigone I carry—
a woman whose name is a charm
and a bond that dissolves in the slate-grey
vernacular of this ocean—the way a scar
is rubbed clean into the skin,
the way the seam in the sheet of ice
fades into the industry
of movement and hue and light.
The struggle is not to repeat
the struggles of the body, like those acids,
those god-like chemicals that will turn me
into forms of what I am.
The struggle is to remain just one man
with ten or twelve hearts
beating in the landless dark.

What the Sea Feeds Us

First a sound like a bone cracking
deep within the body, then
the rising of the ambrosial
chant which is nothing
but the wind and the falling of water.
Every storm's an extraordinary call—
the rapturous northeaster
with its pomp and corrosion.
What's going to happen here
is the invention of the slow
universal solvent, something
nothing can hold—not my sympathy,
not this body, not this bay
where a wave shudders and breaks.

If I had an eye wide enough
I could be both scientist
and evangelist. I could be
a witness to myself.
If I were stormed
with the same political furor
as that grainy bottom of the sea
then I could confuse Armageddon
with the wake of the heart.
And when I open my mouth,
which bitterness is in the wind,
which salt's my own?

A loud nothing, that's what I think
the whole thing will end up being.
Increase and issue and dissolve.

The continent ground into bits
of milky liquid and thin premises
by a storm that is the blackness
at the center of our eyes. It comes from
nowhere and folds our shoulders over
and crosses our arms on our chest—
oh, we're a bad cup, a cultivated pearl.
In this position we shelter our bowels,
the seat of kindness, we suck in.
Whatever it is throws us
so thoroughly into our bodies
that we can taste the sweetbreads
and take and eat them
with our original fists.

After the Storm

A yellow in the sky like the area around a bruise
after the winds that bring the universal thump
around. *It's van Goyen's sky,* we say when we refuse
to make something of it, and it becomes
a low-pitched distance. Why tell the whole story,
why dwell on details when we wake again without a dream
into a world three-quarters cloud and a sea
subdued? We've made absolutely nothing happen. It seems
all artifacts dissolve in breath, in air,
in senses that awake and whelm us,
and in duty, obligation, sentiment, and fear
that is our love, our incubus, our stimulus.
The rosy morning after and the chance
we'll forget, or else the day will glaze our eyes
    like belladonna, like sacraments.

Swan's Riding

1

Hard spiral of a gull in the ceremony of meat,
a coiling as exacting as a theory,
arithmetic and dreamy, and like a theory

full of holes, full of faithless leaks.
There's only so much zen and measurement
before the eye teeth, before the small, exigent

arc described by the flight of hand
to mouth where the emptiness gets stopped
by the perishable again and again

and the imagination can't produce work
that's close to this morning's spark
and elegance—its emerald and rosy-flesh

color, its red robes and its ermine:
hefty chief magistrate with his death sentence
that is carried out as the gull drops

to the shore and grubs and rips
at the bloodless thing in the name of
our hunger, our lowest form of love.

2

The sun out of the sea this morning
impossible to look at, something white,
ignited—a light that burns what I've seen
into place. Even when I close my eyes
it flashes back the phantom, complementary day
of mauve and blue or another day
in a gas station in Zionsgrove, Pennsylvania—
the closest I've come this far to ash.
There a visored, smoke-eyed individual
arc-welded the underbody of the Ford
to the fumes of gasoline to the four
empty chambers of my heart. For an instant
we were brilliant, yoked in a firesack
that lit every fitting, hose, each excruciating
part, but just for that instant,
and our clothes flared but did not burn
while a voice spoke once and loudly, WHOM.
Then I went on somewhere, got something
to eat, slept.

Later, I learned I was singed
as I rubbed my hands in telling
and retelling this dumb show,
this miracle play of threat
and endurance. I lost that fringe
of hair that sometimes glows in photographs
when the light is behind the subject,
and I lost some of my mammalian tenderness
and the language of that loss.
In this picture, I'm the wick,
the bent and flimsy thing
that's neither fuel nor flame.

3

What was it that made us turn
at the edge of the ocean
from our work, our rowing and destination,

our cooking, our documents
and unglorified sorrow of the body
to see it—the swan

rearing up, about our size, masked,
mute, slender in a way we'll never be,
and buoyant and enormously white?

And what was it that made us
give that element it floated on
a name—*the swan's riding:*

the sea, that beleaguered agency
we came across, back breaker,
depth, waste, main?

Even the fisherman I meet admits to me
he turns his eyes from the sea
to the fish so he won't go crazy.

But in the fish eye and the silver
flank there's something breathing.
Even the black rubber boots,

mister Portuguese, are brilliant
with the sheen of feeding,
an equation of mouth and eye

that links the most dutiful
and arty with the daily pain:
water and wafer and a mindless keening.

III

Geometry and Sea Air

It took two days at the beach this spring
for me to remember these things.
First, the body is two-thirds of the way

towards being the selfless thing
that contains both the dead and the fishes.
We're almost home—if we mean that place

we left under duress and now no longer exists
for us to return to, the endless horizontal
without the underworld or otherworldly axis to fix us.

We're exiles, I remembered; we're in some portion
Armenian, and although the body is not the sea,
the sea can be, actually, wine-dark, brilliant, a pedant

in the way it belabors every single point
it touches the way Proust would belabor
the steeples of the churches in Combray,

how they were one day a brown velvet
and the next a jagged flint or flame
but finally something ordinary

and intoxicating, yet an utter authority
of light and bulk like the ocean, nothing trimmed
of its possibility, unafraid of what it is.

It is the second thing—
the prescription given to Keats
on his last voyage from Gravesend

to Naples—*Geometry & Sea Air*
to put a little ballast in your life—
that I remember in the way I sometimes

wish myself away—to give Keats,
for instance, my lungs; to give my marrow
to make blood in the bones

of a friend. That's an oceanic wish,
a happy obliteration—to give every word
for something that works, one word

for one flesh, a calculus of remembering,
a ballast of all the fluids, a ship come in,
a gift of something.

for Tom Sleigh

The Higher Beauties

For the present I have this body
which is just a further way of remembering—
a meaty word. I roll in my sheet,
a bad mammal singing
the subjunctive song of her body,
my memory, my heat, my curse for unselfing.
I crush the accidence still in her teeth.
I turn in my dream. I turn in my reasoning
sleep. To be kissed-off for the higher
beauties, that speech, that's one grievance
I keep alive in my fur, in the *were*
and the *if* I live in since. . . .
This flesh is an enchantment and a solemn vow
broken, this heart beats like a baying hound.

Signorelli's *Last Judgment*, the Blessed

It's a moment coming out of sleep
or deep within the strenuous dream of another
when the body keeps
hold of the celestial. The whir
you heard, was it wings in the ceiling?
Was it the emphasis of cloth
falling from the hips of the awakening
dead? It's that moment when you're lost
but for the body's roundnesses, the balance
of its masses that present the sensible.
Your forehead aches for the corona, the dense
and aspiring eye opens to a place impossible
to place except once in the utopian sleep
and once in the battery of love
when the body opens to heaven and others and moves.

for Cleopatra Mathis

Rooms of Ingres

I'm the illiterate lover, the dumb fuck
in the too, too solid Paris of fact.
I lug in my unseemly baggage, the uninstructed
lust. Mud on my shoes, my hat in my lap.
I'm learning my spot on your still life
of metals and fabrics—the tufted velvet, glass, and all
the jewels whose flawless blues are mirrored in
   handkerchiefs
you let fall and in the coral stitch of the crewel
work of your cloak. Hot house, upholstered, this room.
The fans unfluttered, the chin vapid of wrinkles, the vase
with its vain empire waist. Oh woman of the medium,
the technique, I loved you and your silk, cold gold, and
   brocade.
In my improper case I pack the stuff of billet-doux.
Madame Moitessier, I have no words for you.

Eyes

From their skeletal holes and from their puffy folds
of flesh, two eyes, vitrified, myopic, and membraned
like a dog's with the faint likeness of what appears to be
a man—two men, a small motherwarm pair of enemies
or the most promiscuous and full-lipped of lovers.
We are, are we not, made entirely of light?
So the body makes a pocket in the black
black center, a covenant with our ignorance,
at the point where all this science starts
in the repetitious, horribly incongrous surfaces
and sights. Around these pits, two irises, a colorless
brown like the surname, Smith, the color of the flower
in its dying. And in three seconds, a blink,
a blindness, an elegy, a blink. When things rise
again we're granted amnesty from the unseen moments
in the dark that must add up to a year's worth of death
in a lifetime. There's mortality in their namesakes—
the noose, the nodes of the exhumed root, the storm's
center, the bloody piece of beef—but there's another
eye whose offspring is the wings of butterflies,
the nugget, the hard way to heaven through a needle.
Here's Caliban and Ariel, here's mud in your eye,
half stars in the other. And here in the corners,
the scum of looking and the famous veil of tears
as if the scraps of each bright thing we see
can be so glued, a cairn, a souvenir, or stored away
like the provisional sleep cake we wake to.
Oh these embryos aswim in their humors, these defective
child emperors of emptiness and light who dream away
their kingdoms in the good dark third of life.

Awake they call up all the phantoms, the vagabonds,
the fugitives—that hound with its teeth
in my daughter's cheek, the fifteen black stitches,
or that brain-shaped cloud that mushrooms up
from the film of 1945, from apertures in sleep.
If I could only keep them shut and joyous
as in kissing, if I could only keep them
in their purses like marsupials or blood money.

Mine are the bloodshot whites.
And I could say the same for my race
and generation, The Wrathful and the Sullen,
the Spiritual Bandits, the plain dumb white guys
in our one circle of hell which looks almost like
the bus terminal in Philadelphia where on the wall
under the profligate jokes, the goodtimes, the false
and perjurous phone numbers, I search the hagiography
to find the names of my brothers and sisters—Ah,
the Maniac Drifters! To turn this persistent image
upside down, to pavilion the dust, to Atlas
the bulk of the splendorous, venal world,
my eyes draw blood from the heart.
Can this in any way explain us? Hookworms and witnesses?
Host of a violent, uncivil light? Like acetylene,
like continuing under the shattered bulb of Guernica?
And this bloody business shows in the eyes
as tiny lightning, red maps of areas remote, canals
on Mars, Khe Sahn, the provinces of some other America.
Under a brow that's the vestige of the hunt, furred
blond-brown, under two lips that rasp instead of rinse,
tearless, the doctor says—I'm astonished I can see
at all—my eyes more vulva than window to the soul,
although some lesser thing, some fallen angel,

enters, miraculously, these under-windows.
It's just that miracle my lashes clap for,
the sacrilege of this engendering, this vaudeville
of their nervous, soundless applause.

for Denis Johnson

A Small Sing of My Cupidity

As I perish into the work
of kissing the dark awake,

I curl around the bruise
of the malcontents of summer,

the violet seethe of the blackbird,
a tug from that end of the spectrum.

I hug all the cold forms
and the roach and the will-o-the-wisp,

though I don't have her touch,
her zero of the flesh,

in my sleep I breathe
her wealth of broken O's:

her collar bones, the filament
of her black hair, the arch of her back

the want in the press of her seal
in my right hand and forehead.

Meridian Street

The street, rain black, iridescent
from the sheen of oils. Two parallel lines
across the frame of the window.

I was schooled like this—the seasons
through a hole, the local and the steadfast
banded by lines—the view of the U.S.

Federal Penitentiary of Lewisburg, Pennsylvania,
my alma mater, where loss was promise
if you stared hard enough, where this pastime

went beyond distraction to the fetish
of things, the fondling of anything, anything—
a pigeon, a shoe—the devotion of a man

to that isolate, undeviating
outpouring of all the forces of one life—
as if a jet of water could be first quartered,

then metered, then fountained to an understanding
of the rains of his city, Buffalo or Oakland
or the slick of a street in St. Louis, or,

heaven forbid a brother being caught there,
Galveston or somewhere north of Boston,
or in that thirty-four-hundred block of Meridian

in Philadelphia where the rain fell for me,
first righteous, *we need it*, I would say, as if I could
speak for anyone more than this passive, wind-pulled

prisoner that I was and was to be. In two days
the rain was universally grey, in three
a slate dropped on the foot, a wrong

the kind St. Paul swore would be a sin
against the Holy Ghost in days four and five.
The streets flooded, bricks scummed

with the high water, no way out, no way back,
just the score of this attention,
the coin and spoils of this arrest.

When the Rapture Comes

I must study politics and war so that my sons may . . .
study mathematics . . . in order to give their children a
right to study painting, poetry, music, architecture.
    —JOHN ADAMS TO HIS WIFE ABIGAIL

So that my daughter may someday study
painting, poetry, music, architecture,
I study the windows of the houses

of men that I hate,
how they receive the gem's benefit
after the five-days' rain—

an equity of the invisible, the brittle,
and the light that makes these panes
shocked with the world like the newly slain-

in-the-spirit who wants heaven
right now and gets it
through the touch on the temples

and falls down loudly and gets up
no longer halt or lame
with the eyes rolled up in the head.

Who's to say what's ecstasy
and what needs the miracle put to it
like a smokeless forty-four?

Some of these men, Megan,
ought to be shot. I said that,
and what I meant was

that exactly. I don't know
which one of us it will be,
but one of us will have to name names:

The Violent Against Silence,
The Treacherous Against the Next Breath . . .
I want one of us to be armed

and dangerous with a rage
pure and faceted with power. I want one of us
to be ready when the rapture comes—

that's the slogan of the violently
certain. I want one of us to be that sure,
and to rectify or at least get even.

We're nobody's legislators, nobody's voice
unless we can break the knees
of our own devices the way light

is broken into garnet and diamond
and the green light of tourmaline
which is not the color of money.

Then I can see a poetry
as durable and flagrant as hatred,
a hatred I can study or play.

Ode

Turn

I want to tell you on this first day
of bona fide sun in New York,
June, just what it is to measure
and itch, to dream toward the tender
boundaries in this hot property.
Air, flesh, the light emotional,
delux. The heart enlarges
so that its thousand chambers burst
the difference between enterprise
and despair. In the sun's country
all the citizens are foreign—
that vast man in plum-skin
slacks who brothers me
and the Asian who has no juice
inside him. I want to tell you
about each one with the injured air
in his lungs and these Egyptians
the sun generates—scarabs,
crocodelians, the bright winged things

Counterturn

with their gorgeous, historical beauty.
They're sensational, gangsterous and vain—
strong arms of the adorable.
I want that beautiful something in a portion
that won't break my heart—a thread,
a single wing of the paper, a chestnut
in its smoke, a glint, an ort

of all the possible. Then I could come closer.
I could stand in the doorways
and next to the tunnels and towers.
I'd listen to the traffic's hosannahs,
and before I'd embrace any one
of these perishable things,
I'd watch whole buckets of the plagiarized
white iris brown in the sun
no matter what I would do
or what I would not do
which sounds like a prayer

Stand

a necrophiliac would make
to arrest those things he would love.
All allegiance cuffs and chafes.
These are the rigors of our devotion.
And the bodies are everywhere
in the stations, in the zones,
embalmed in the smells of the blocks.
I've seen them in the neoclassical
junkyards of the Bronx and in all the boroughs.
I loved once.
And I tell you with that part of me
that remembers the economy
of want and be-wanted, the splendid
accounting of the body's filaments,
the collar bones, the delicate bones
of the wrists. This is how I resist.

Turn

And when I turn away from grief
I turn to grief again, this voice

is Dante's after his swoon
from the carnal—the two lovers
in their eternal flight in the torn sky
and his awakening in the rain
of the foul third circle of Hell,
the filth of the Florence he loved.
It's that miserable proximity
of lust and gluttony—the storm
and its attendant hail that makes me
think my appetite is in this same order:
desire, then a dizziness,
then a dizzying desire to love
all the stinking things I wallow in.
In it I can almost taste myself.

Counterturn

It's like trying to meditate
with shit in my mouth.
The glut of the metropolis
makes any word devout
or criminal. Like the sea,
anything you say is occasional
and true. The sky today is that same
blue I once saw over the ocean
and a word there falls as unheard
in the waves as in the whir
of the city's tachycardia.
I want to tell you what it is
to be in this hot jacket, target,
this sloppy house with its almost
miraculous kitchen, its cults.
But what can I say that's not the self?
And what voice can I give it
beside the ring of my conviction

Stand

that insists that I love it
before it dies with the kind of love
that's safe from the sun
and the moon's jurisprudence,
that's safe from the oblivion
of her and him? It's a mighty power,
I know, that can,
like the skinniest inmate
of the penitentiary, blow for hours
a single fugue on his alto sax
against the unremitting wall.
Who knows at the height
of his strenuous riff
if he plans an escape
in the cracks he invents,
or protracts the inevitable hook
at the end of the question
or just echoes in the story
of his unenlightened crimes?